THE GOOD SHEPHERD

Storybook

Georgie Adams *Illustrated by* Peter Utton

BROADMAN
& HOLMAN
PUBLISHERS

With fondest memories of Constance Adams—G.A.

To my mum Lucy, and the grandchildren—P.U.

Published in 1999 by Broadman & Holman Publishers
Nashville, Tennessee
First published in Great Britain in 1999
by Orion Children's Books
a division of the Orion Publishing Group Ltd
Orion House
5 Upper St Martin's Lane
London WC2H 9EA

Text copyright © Georgie Adams 1999
Illustrations copyright © Peter Utton 1999
Designed by Ian Butterworth

A catalog record for this book is available from the Library of Congress.

Printed in Italy
ISBN 0805419608

Contents

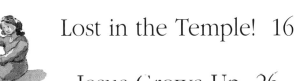

Foreword

The stories in this book are from the part of the Bible called the New Testament. They are all about Jesus, the Son of God. They are much loved stories such as *The Marvelous Catch of Fish, Water Changed into Wine,* and *The Story of the Sower.* Remember, Jesus lived in Palestine nearly two thousand years ago, so you see these stories have been around for a very long time!

At first everything Jesus said and did was simply talked about by people who had seen and heard him. Jesus spent much of his time teaching his disciples—the twelve special friends who had chosen to follow him—to do just that. He wanted everyone to love and obey God, and taught them how to change their ways and live better lives.

Often when Jesus was trying to tell people about himself, he told stories to help them understand. In the story of *The Good Shepherd,* Jesus said he was like a shepherd looking after the sheep in his flock. Or, when people asked him questions about how they might enter heaven, Jesus told them they had to be like children and trust him. "The kingdom of God belongs to little children," he said. "God is your heavenly Father, and you are all his children."

Stories and sayings such as these would have been passed from one family to the next, in the way that Bible stories from the Old Testament had been handed down for hundreds of years, long before Jesus was born.

In time everything was written down, and put together to make the Bible. But the way the stories were written is not always easy to read. So I have retold some of the stories in this book, imagining what it would have been like for the men, women, and children who were with Jesus, so many years ago. Some stories are full of danger and excitement; others tell of miracles, and the love Jesus had for everyone around him. All of them are wonderful, mysterious stories I hope you will enjoy!

Georgie Adams

Jesus was born in Bethlehem, in a country called Judea, a long time ago. His parents, Mary and Joseph, loved him very much. All parents think their babies are special, but Jesus really was the most important baby ever. Even before he was born, an angel had told Mary that her baby was the Son of God. So you see how special he was?

But from the very beginning of his life, baby Jesus was in great danger. King Herod, who ruled Judea at that time, heard that this tiny baby was to be the King of the Jews. And that made him jealous. Herod didn't want anyone else ruling his land, so he ordered his army to find Jesus—and kill him!

One night, just before Herod's soldiers came marching into Bethlehem, Joseph had a dream. In his dream an angel told him about the king's wicked plan.

"You must escape tonight!" said the angel. "Take Mary and the child to Egypt. You can hide there safely."

Joseph woke Mary at once. She wrapped Jesus in warm blankets, and Joseph saddled the donkey. Then they crept, quiet as mice, out of the town. It was the middle of the night. Mary clutched her precious baby tightly in her arms, and hoped he wouldn't cry. She was afraid they might be seen.

Bethlehem was built
high up in the Judean hills. At
first Joseph led the donkey through
leafy olive groves, down a steep twisty
road, away from the town. They probably
walked all that night, stopping to rest for a while at
an inn the next day. Traveling with a baby was difficult,
Mary had to feed and care for Jesus every few hours.

Their journey was easier once they reached the coast. The Romans had built an excellent new road, wide and straight for miles. After that they had to cross the scorching desert. It was a long and dangerous journey, because sometimes thieves tried to rob people traveling on the road.

Mary and Joseph may have gone some of the way with other travelers. It was safer to walk in a group. There would have been rich merchants in mule carts, loaded with spices. Or traders on camels, carrying beautiful rugs, all going to the Egyptian markets to sell their goods.

At last, Mary and Joseph reached Egypt, and found somewhere to stay. They hadn't been there long when they heard that King Herod had died. The angel, who had warned Joseph to escape from Bethlehem, came to him again in another dream. He told him it was safe to return home.

So Mary, Joseph, and Jesus left Egypt. But instead of going back to Bethlehem, Joseph took the road up into the green hills around the Sea of Galilee. And at a village called Nazareth, they stopped and made their home.

Lost in the Temple!

Most of the stories in the Bible are about Jesus when he was thirty years old. There are very few that were written about him as a child, so we shall just have to imagine what it was like for Jesus, growing up in Nazareth.

At this time, all Jewish boys began school when they were six. Girls didn't go to school then! They stayed at home, and were taught the very strict rules about cooking and cleaning by their mothers.

Girls also learned to spin and weave. And every mother, like Mary, would have told her children wonderful Bible stories about God and his people. Exciting stories about Noah's ark, Moses crossing the Red Sea, or David fighting Goliath—which you'll find in the part of the Bible called the Old Testament.

Jesus would have gone to school six days a week in Nazareth, at the synagogue—a Jewish place of prayer. His teacher, the rabbi, would have taught the class how to write the Hebrew alphabet, and learn God's law by heart. One of the most important laws Jesus learned was to obey his parents. Jesus tried hard to do what Mary and Joseph told him to do.

And when school was finished for the day, Jesus would have gone to play with his friends—a game of hoops or marbles were as popular with children then as they are now. Or perhaps Joseph, who was a carpenter, showed Jesus how to use carpentry tools, to make toys out of wood. Who knows? Joseph may have helped Jesus chisel and carve a Noah's ark, with all the animals inside.

There is one story in the Bible about Jesus when he was twelve years old. It happened at the time of a special festival called Passover, which Jewish families celebrate once a year. They remember a time when God 'passed over' the homes of his people and kept them safe, in the days when Moses lived.

It was springtime. Mary and Joseph were taking Jesus to Jerusalem for the Passover festival for the first time. He was old enough now, and lots of his friends were going. They set off from Nazareth with many other families, full of excited chatter.

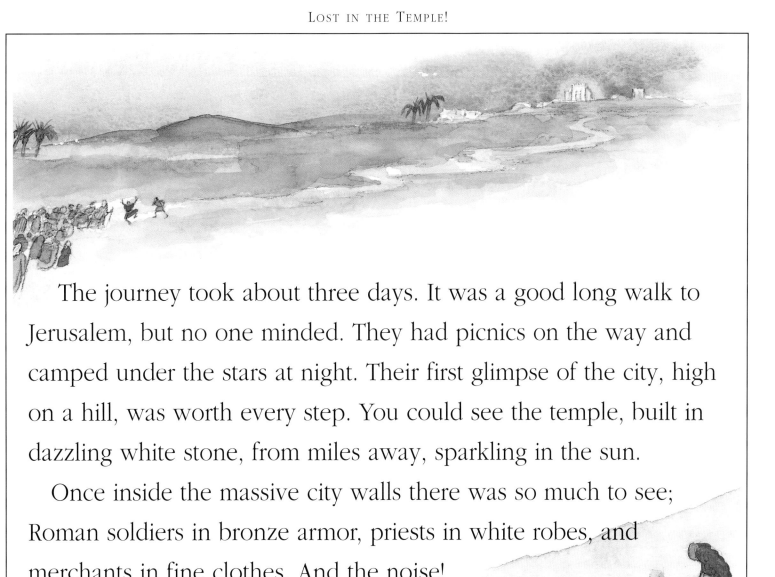

The journey took about three days. It was a good long walk to Jerusalem, but no one minded. They had picnics on the way and camped under the stars at night. Their first glimpse of the city, high on a hill, was worth every step. You could see the temple, built in dazzling white stone, from miles away, sparkling in the sun.

Once inside the massive city walls there was so much to see; Roman soldiers in bronze armor, priests in white robes, and merchants in fine clothes. And the noise! Crowds jostled and shouted in the busy street markets.

Jesus couldn't wait to see the temple.

"Come on then," said Joseph, "but stay close to me, or you'll get lost."

Joseph knew a way through the narrow streets and along dark passageways. Mary and Jesus followed him as he climbed stone steps to a wide outer courtyard . . . and there stood the temple, behind gateways, battlements, and giant marble columns.

It was magnificent.

The Passover festival lasted for a whole week. Mary and Joseph often went to the temple to worship, and Jesus soon got to know his way around. He felt strangely at home there; he wandered around courtyards full of worshippers, and among groups of people listening to rabbis.

All too soon it was time to return to Nazareth. There was quite a crowd going that way, and Mary and Joseph joined them at the city gate. Mary couldn't see Jesus.

"Don't worry," said Joseph, "he'll be tagging along with his friends."

And so they set off.

Towards evening, everyone got ready to camp for the night. Mary and Joseph looked around for Jesus, but they couldn't find him. They were anxious. No one had seen him as they walked along that day. Who had seen him last? Had he left Jerusalem? One thing seemed certain. Jesus was missing!

Early the next morning Mary and Joseph hurried back to the city. They felt sick with worry. For two days they searched for Jesus, asking anyone if they had seen a twelve-year-old boy wandering alone. On the third day they met someone who *had* seen a young boy—in the temple.

"I noticed him because I saw him talking to the teachers and rabbis," said the man. "He was asking lots of questions."

Mary and Joseph thanked him and ran to the temple. Could it have been Jesus? Where was he now? They rushed through the courtyards, from one group of people to another until . . .

There he was! He was sitting with some grey-bearded wise men, talking about religion. The teachers were amazed that a boy of his age could have so much understanding of God.

Well, of course, Mary and Joseph were very happy to see Jesus again, but they were cross too.

"How could you do this?" scolded Mary. "We have been looking everywhere for you!"

Jesus was surprised that they hadn't looked in the temple first.

"Didn't you know that I would be in my Father's house?" he said.

It seemed a strange thing to say. Mary and Joseph didn't understand then that Jesus was talking about God, his Father in heaven. Mary thought about his words, but said nothing more. At that moment, all they could think about was the journey back to Nazareth, and home.

Jesus Grows Up

The Bible doesn't tell us anything about Jesus as a young man, which is a pity. It is most likely that he learned to be a carpenter like Joseph, in the family workshop in Nazareth.

Joseph would have taught Jesus how to use carpentry tools properly, to make furniture such as chairs, tables, and beds. Carpenters in those days were also kept busy making doors and roof-beams for houses, so Jesus would have been used to lifting heavy pieces of timber.

When Joseph died, Jesus probably stayed at home to look after his mother. As a skilled craftsman, he would have found plenty of work around Galilee, earning money for both of them to live on.

The Marvelous Catch of Fish

Jesus was about thirty years old when he began his work for God. He said he was the Son of God, sent by his heavenly Father to show how people should live.

But Jesus needed some friends to help him—the Bible calls them disciples. This story tells you about the very first men Jesus chose to follow him.

Jesus went to live at a town called Capernaum, by the Sea of Galilee. The sea was really an enormous lake, so big that it would take days to sail around it. Jesus often walked along the shore. There were always lots of fishing boats around, and he had made friends with some of the fishermen.

One morning he saw four of them together. There was Simon and his brother, Andrew, hauling in their boat. James and John were mending their nets. None of them looked happy.

"We've been fishing all night," grumbled Simon, "and we haven't caught a thing. Not one flapping fish."

While Jesus was there some people gathered round, and he talked to them about God. More and more people came to listen until there was quite a crowd.

"Speak up!" said someone at the back. "We can't hear."

So Jesus asked Simon to help.

"Push your boat a little way into the water," he said. "I'll speak from there."

So Simon and Andrew pushed the boat over the pebbles and into the lake. Then Jesus stood up in the boat and spoke to everyone waiting on the shore. It was much better. He spent all day talking to them. By late afternoon the sun was slipping down behind the hills, and people began to go home.

Simon and Andrew were about to head
the boat back to the shore, when Jesus said,
"Go out into deeper water, and let down
your nets."

Simon was a bit doubtful. After all, they
had caught nothing the night before. But he
trusted Jesus.

"All right," he said. "If you say so, we will."

Andrew set the sail and they headed out into deeper water. When they had gone far enough, Simon flung the nets overboard. SPLASH!

As the nets sank, Simon and Andrew looked over the side of the boat. They could hardly believe what they saw. Hundreds of darting silver fish came swimming by. Fish of every shape and size swirled around the boat. In no time, their nets were full. Andrew was the first to realize they weren't dreaming.

"Heave ho!" he shouted.

It was all the two fishermen could do to pull in the catch, without sinking the boat. James and John were watching them from another boat.

"Come and help," yelled Simon.

I am sure Jesus helped too. And when James and John came alongside, there were as many fish as before for them to fill their own nets.

As the fishermen returned to the shore, Simon knew that this had been no ordinary catch. Jesus had made it happen. He could do wonderful things. Later, while they were sorting and cleaning the fish, Jesus said to them,

"Leave your fishing nets and come with me. I will teach you to fish for people, so that they may know and love God."

That is how Simon, Andrew, James, and John left their boats to start a new life with Jesus. And from that day on, Simon was known by another name: Jesus called him Peter, which means "a rock."

Water Changed into Wine

Little Sarah was very excited. Her big sister, Ruth, had gotten married and they were having a big wedding party. Wedding feasts then could last for a whole week.

Sarah had been looking forward to the wedding for months, ever since Ruth and her bridegroom, David, had promised to marry. They had given each other rings at a special ceremony, and Ruth's father was paid some money for his daughter (known as 'the bride price') which was the custom. As soon as David had found a house, the wedding was arranged. It was being held at a town called Cana, not far from Nazareth.

Sarah and her friends were having a wonderful time. There was delicious food to eat, and wine to drink. Sarah laughed to see some of the guests trying to dance to the music.

Day after day, more and more guests came to see the bride and bridegroom. David's parents were kept busy preparing food, and making sure there was enough to drink. After a few days, David's father looked worried, and Sarah overheard him say,

"We're running out of wine. What shall we do?"

It happened that Jesus, his mother, Mary, and all the disciples
had been invited to the wedding. By now Jesus had twelve
disciples, and they all came along. There was Peter (the rock) and
his brother, Andrew; James and John; Philip, Bartholomew, Thomas
and Matthew; another man named James; Thaddaeus, Simon, and
last of all, Judas Iscariot.

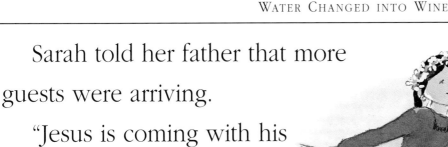

Sarah told her father that more guests were arriving.

"Jesus is coming with his friends," she said.

They arrived just as the wine ran out. Mary noticed it first and whispered to Jesus,

"They have no wine left! Can you do something?"

Mary believed he could help. So she said to one of the servants,

"Do whatever he tells you."

Quietly Jesus spoke to the servant, and pointed to six large water jars, which could hold many gallons of water.

"Fill those jars with water," he said. "Then pour some out and take it to the bridegroom's best friend."

The servant found some others to help, and they filled each jar to the brim. Sarah watched as they poured some into a smaller jug.

"May I carry it?" she asked.

The servant said she could. So Sarah carefully took the jug to David's friend. He was sitting with David and Ruth at the table. He took one sip, smacked his lips and said,

"Hm! This *is* a good wine."

And because it was so good, he got up and made a speech, to thank David and his family.

"You are most generous," he said. "Most people serve the best wine first, and the not so good wine at the end of the wedding. You have saved the best until last!"

Sarah may not have understood what really happened that day, but the twelve disciples did. They knew how special Jesus was. He had changed the water into wine, to make the wedding a happy one. And from that day, they believed he would change the way people lived too.

One day Jesus was walking with his disciples in the high hills, overlooking the Sea of Galilee. As usual he was followed by many people—mothers with their babies, children, young men and old—all hoping to hear Jesus speak.

When they were halfway up a mountain, Jesus stopped and sat down.

"Listen," he said. "God wants us to love him and to love one another, not just obey rules."

He was talking about the laws God had given Moses hundreds of years before. Jesus didn't mean people shouldn't obey those laws, but he did try to explain what God *really* meant by them. Some religious teachers had added lots more rules, and keeping every one of them made life very difficult.

Whenever Jesus spoke about God, he tried to say things in a way everyone would understand. So he thought for a while and said,

"God wants you to be like him. Every day, try living in a way you know would please him. Be a good example to others. Shine like a lamp, so that everyone can see you are trying to obey God."

While Jesus spoke, some children were playing on the hill. They were rolling down a slope, having fun. Perhaps seeing that happy group of friends together reminded him of one law, which needed to be thought about in a different way.

"You've been told that as long as you love your friends, you can hate your enemies," he said. "Well, it's easy to love friends but, I say God wants us to love our enemies too. Try to think like God. After all, he gives the sun and rain to everyone, good and bad."

The disciples sitting nearby nodded. They understood that to be kind to those they didn't like would be hard, but they could see Jesus was right.

Jesus taught them many things that day. One of them was about prayer.

"When you pray," he said, "do it quietly, on your own. Don't be like the show-offs who stand up in the temple or on street corners where they can be seen. Go to your room and talk to God there. He'll hear your prayers. And there's no need to use words you don't understand, or make your prayers long. Anyway, your Father in heaven knows what you need, before you even ask."

Then Jesus put his hands together, closed his eyes and taught them how to pray. It is the prayer we know as the Lord's Prayer:

Our Father in heaven,
hallowed be your name,
your kingdom come,
your will be done,
on earth as in heaven.
Give us today our daily bread.
Forgive us our sins
as we forgive those who sin against us.
Lead us not into temptation
but deliver us from evil.
For the kingdom, the power, and the glory are yours,
now and for ever. Amen.

When he had finished praying, Jesus spoke of other things. He told everyone not to worry so much about having enough food to eat, or clothes to wear. They should trust God more and believe he will look after them.

"Look at the birds," he said. "They don't sow seeds, or cut corn and store it in a barn, but God cares for them, doesn't he?"

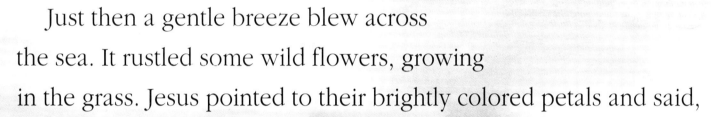

Just then a gentle breeze blew across the sea. It rustled some wild flowers, growing in the grass. Jesus pointed to their brightly colored petals and said, "See those beautiful flowers? They don't sew their own clothes! But, I tell you, even the great King Solomon with all his money never had such fine things to wear. So if God clothes the flowers and feeds the birds—imagine how much more he will do for you. You just have to trust him."

Then Jesus turned to some parents who were there, and asked them, "Would any of you give your children a stone when they asked for bread? Or a snake if they asked for some fish?"

When they looked puzzled and shook their heads he said,

"Of course not! However bad you are, you would give good things to your children. And God is like that too. You are all his children, so just think how much more your heavenly Father will give you, if you ask him."

Jesus ended his teaching that day by telling everyone a story. It went something like this:

"If you hear my words and obey them, you'll be like the wise man who built his house on rock. The rain came pouring down, the wind blew, and floods came swirling round the door. The wise man's house stood up to all that terrible weather, because he had built it on solid rock."

Jesus looked around. Everyone was listening, so he went on.

"But those who hear me, and *don't* do as I say, will be like the foolish man. He built his house on sand. When the storm came, and the flood waters rose up around his windows, his house came tumbling down. The shifting sand gave way beneath it, and the house fell with a terrible crash!"

It didn't take people long to figure out what this story really meant. If they did as Jesus had taught them, they would be strong. His words were like the rock in the story.

Jesus Heals the Sick

Jesus was back in Capernaum. Not only was he a wonderful teacher, but he could make sick people well again.

One day while Jesus was walking in the town, a man with a dreadful skin disease saw him. He came right up to Jesus, knelt down at his feet and said,

"Master, if you want to, you can make me well."

Now this was an amazing thing to say because the man was a leper. He had been suffering with horrible sores on his arms and legs for years. No doctor had been able to cure him, but the leper believed Jesus could.

Jesus took pity on him at once. He could see how the man trusted him.

"I will help you," he said. "Be well!"

The man's sores vanished. He was completely cured. Jesus asked the man not to tell anyone about what had happened. He had a feeling some Jewish leaders would hear about it, and make trouble. The Pharisees and religious teachers had been wanting to get Jesus arrested for some time. They were jealous that so many ordinary people loved Jesus, and believed him to be the Son of God. So Jesus told the man to go straight to his priest, show that he was healthy, and to give an offering to God. That was the law.

Well, the man did that but he just couldn't resist telling his friends how Jesus had healed him. The news spread like wildfire. From then on, the little house where Jesus lived was always full of people, wanting to be with him.

It was like that on the day this next miracle happened. The Bible doesn't tell us exactly who was in the house, apart from some of those troublesome religious leaders I told you about. People had come from all over Galilee, and as far away as Jerusalem, to hear what Jesus had to say. I like to think that a little boy named Joshua may have been there that day, and saw what happened . . .

Joshua lived across the street, selling pots, bowls, and water jugs his father had made. On this particular day, Joshua sat dreaming in the sun. No one was buying any pots, they were far too busy talking to Jesus in the house across the street.

Suddenly, Joshua was startled by some men shouting. He looked up and saw four young men hurrying along the street. They were carrying a friend on a stretcher. The poor man was paralyzed and couldn't walk.

"Make way! Make way!" cried the men, pushing their way through the crowd.

They stopped outside the house where Jesus was. There were so many people, they couldn't get near the door.

"We'll have to go up to the roof!" said one of the stretcher bearers.

"Which way?" asked another.

"There," shouted Joshua. He pointed to some stone steps at the side of the house.

Like most houses in Capernaum, this one had a flat roof. It was made of wooden beams, plastered with a mixture of clay and straw, a good place to sleep out on hot nights. Joshua watched as the men struggled to carry the stretcher up the steps. What was going on?

His curiosity got the better of him. He ran across the street and climbed on to the roof, after them. To his great surprise he found the four men ripping up the plaster, and tearing at the wood with their bare hands. They were making a hole in the roof!

When it was big enough, they tied strips of cloth to the stretcher, and carefully lowered it into the room below where Jesus was talking. They peered through the hole, and saw Jesus bending over the sick man. The Bible tells us what happened next.

Jesus knew how much faith this man had in him, so he said, "Your sins are forgiven."

Now, that really upset the troublesome teachers who were listening. They said only God could forgive sins. But Jesus knew what they were thinking. He told them he *did* have the right to forgive people, and he showed it was true by healing the paralyzed man.

"Get up," said Jesus. "Pick up your bed and go home."

To everyone's astonishment, the man who couldn't move a muscle, got up and walked out of the house! It was a miracle. No one had ever seen anything like it.

"We have seen something marvelous today," they all said.

And I'm sure young Joshua agreed.

The Story of the Sower

Farming was an important part of everyday life in Judea. Farmers provided all kinds of fruit and vegetables such as apples, grapes, olives, beans, and onions. They also grew crops of wheat and barley.

The farmer plowed his fields in winter. He used a simple wooden plow to break down lumps of earth into fine, crumbly soil, ready for sowing. The plow was usually pulled by two oxen, because in those days there were no tractors.

In spring, wheat or barley was sown. The farmer walked up and down each field, scattering handfuls of seed from a basket. After a few weeks the first green shoots appeared, and the rain and warm sunshine helped the plants to grow.

At harvest time the whole family joined in. First the men cut the crop with sickles, made of iron. Then the women and children threshed it, beating the ripe grains from the stalks. And on windy days, they all worked hard winnowing or tossing grains in the air. The breeze blew away the light, papery husks, leaving the heavier golden grains behind. The wheat grains were ground into flour to make bread.

Jesus would have known about these things. One day while he was teaching, he told people a story about a farmer—the Bible calls him a sower. It went something like this:

"Listen," said Jesus. "There was once a sower who went out to sow . . ."

He walked along scattering seeds, but only some fell on the good, plowed soil. The wind blew a few seeds on to the hard footpath that ran alongside the field. In no time the birds swooped down and ate them. Some seeds fell on rocky ground where there was hardly any soil at all. The seeds sprouted, but the soil wasn't deep enough for their roots. The hot sun soon dried them up. A few seeds fell into thorn bushes, which choked the plants. They didn't produce any grain. But the seeds that fell on good soil produced lots of grain, and the farmer had a fine crop.

Jesus told this story to show the many different ways people listen to God's message. Each part of the story has a special meaning—like a code. Jesus told everyone to listen and learn, as he explained what it meant.

"If you have ears, use them!" he said.

The sower in the story is the person who tells people about God. The seed is God's message about the way he wants us to live. The message is spread among people, like seeds.

The footpath really means hard-hearted people. They hear God's message, but it doesn't sink in. They don't use their ears properly, so the message is wasted, in the same way that some seeds were wasted, and the birds swooped down and ate them. Others are more like the rocky ground; they are pleased to hear about God but, if something goes wrong, they forget all about him. They haven't understood enough for God's words to take root.

Then there are the thorn bushes, or people who crowd out the message with their own worries. They are much too busy making money or buying things, to stop and listen about God.

But people who are like the good soil, listen and *understand* God's message. When those people hear it, the sower will have a very good harvest. They will change their ways, live better lives, and tell others about God, too.

Walking on the Water

There were times when Jesus needed to be alone. Most days he was surrounded by people, working hard, teaching them about God. So quiet times were important to him. He could talk to God in prayer.

One evening Jesus was by the Sea of Galilee. He told his disciples to get in their boat, and go back to Capernaum. He would follow later. As Jesus walked towards the hills to pray, he passed some boys cooking fish over a campfire. He smiled and waved at them. He could remember doing that as a boy.

Now I told you the Sea of Galilee is really a big lake, many miles long and wide. The local fishermen knew these waters well; one minute the lake was as calm as a pond, the next, a sudden squall would whip the waters into gigantic waves. That is what happened in this story.

The twelve disciples were in the boat—Peter, Philip, Andrew, and all the others. At first it was very peaceful rowing across the lake. The slow dip and splash of the oars probably sent some of them to sleep. But as the sun slipped down behind the hills, a strong breeze blew up. It rippled the waters and, before long, a fierce wind turned those ripples into waves.

When they got to the middle of the lake, a fierce storm had broke out. But there was no turning back! Huge waves dashed over the side of the boat, which was very frightening. Even the most experienced fishermen among them were afraid. They did their best to keep the boat on course.
Some pulled on the oars, while
others bailed out the water.

By early morning they were exhausted.
They had been battling the storm all night.
Peter strained his eyes to see if he could see
land. And, at that moment, he saw the strangest thing.
Something or *someone* was walking on the water.

They all looked and couldn't believe their eyes. It was Jesus
walking towards them. The disciples were terrified and thought he
was a ghost! So Jesus spoke to them.

"Don't be afraid," he said. "It's me!"

Peter still wasn't sure, and he called out,

"Lord, if it's really you, tell me to come to you."

Then Jesus beckoned to Peter and said, "Come."

Well, Peter was over the side of the boat in no time. He was sure
he could walk to Jesus. But after only a few
steps, Peter lost courage, and started to sink!

"Save me, Lord!" he cried.

Of course Jesus was there quickly.
He held out his hand and grabbed
hold of Peter, who was floundering
in the water.

"Why did you doubt me?" said Jesus.

If Peter's faith had been stronger, he would
have been all right. After they were both back in the boat, the storm
died down. The lake was calm as they rowed back to the shore.
Once again the disciples had seen how powerful Jesus was, and
they believed he was the Son of God.

The Good Shepherd

At the time Jesus was teaching in Galilee, many people kept sheep. They provided meat, milk, and wool—and often lambs were used as sacrifices to God.

Shepherds and shepherdesses took great care of their animals. They taught their children to look after them too. During the day, shepherds would lead their flocks to wherever they could find food and water. Sometimes they walked over many hills to find enough grass for their animals to eat. They were often away from home for days. But the sheep knew their own shepherd so well, they would come when he called. Or, if a young lamb lost its mother and needed to be fed, a shepherdess would carry it home and care for it there.

At night shepherds drove their flocks into sheepfolds, built of stone. Although the sun was burning hot all day, at night it was freezing cold, so shepherds had to wrap themselves in thick blankets to keep warm. Then they would lie down across the entrance, to protect their sheep from leopards and wolves, and watch out for robbers too! So you see a good shepherd had to be brave.

Jesus knew all about shepherds. Sometimes, when he was trying to tell people about himself, Jesus told them stories about shepherds, to help them understand.

Remember I told you about the Pharisees and religious teachers being jealous, always trying to find fault with Jesus? Well, one day Jesus overheard one of those troublesome teachers grumbling to another.

"That man Jesus mixes with dreadful people," he said. "Do you know, I've seen him talking to tax collectors who cheat us out of too much money, and thieves. He even eats with them."

Jesus must have sighed. Couldn't they see that he was doing God's work among the people who needed him most?

"Listen," he said. "If a shepherd had a hundred sheep, and one of them was missing, what would he do? He'd leave the other ninety-nine on the hill, and go and look for the lost one. And, when he had found it, he would carry it home on his shoulder. The shepherd would be so pleased to have found the lost sheep, he'd invite his friends to a party."

Those religious leaders were beginning to get the message, lost sheep were like the rogues Jesus often mixed with.

"I tell you," said Jesus, "God will be more pleased about one wrongdoer who changes his ways and starts to do right, than about ninety-nine law-abiding folks who don't need to!"

Another time Jesus said he was like a good shepherd. In the same way that sheep knew the voice of their shepherd, people would come to know him too. They would know he was the true Son of God. And, if they followed his teaching, they would live their lives as God wanted them to. Jesus said they would become one flock, with one shepherd.

The Lost Coin

There was once a little girl named Rachel who loved her grandmother, Anna, very much. Rachel lived in the same village as Anna, so she visited her grandmother every day.

Sometimes they would sit up on the flat roof of Anna's house, weaving. Anna had taught Rachel how to weave threads on a loom, to make patterned floor mats. And while they sat working, Anna would tell Rachel exciting Bible stories of long ago. Her favorite story was about Joseph and his coat of many colors.

One morning Rachel found her grandmother busily sweeping the floor. Rachel stood in the doorway and coughed. Anna's sweeping was making a lot of dust! Although it was quite dark inside, Rachel saw that her grandmother looked worried.

"What's the matter?" she asked.

"Oh, silly me!" said Anna. "I've dropped a silver coin somewhere. I had ten in this little bag, and now I've lost one."

"I'll help you look for it," said Rachel.

So Anna lit an oil lamp, and they hunted for the coin. Rachel made a game of it. First

she looked under the bed, but the coin wasn't there. Then Anna took the lamp into the dark corners of the room, but she couldn't see the precious coin anywhere.

"It's lost forever," she sighed.

Just then rays of sunlight shone through the open doorway, and Rachel spotted something glinting in the sun. It was the missing silver coin.

"Look," she cried. "I've found it."

Rachel picked it up and gave it to her grandmother. Anna hugged the little girl tight. Then, because she was so happy, she danced with Rachel all around the room. They were making such a noise, some neighbors came to see what all the fuss was about.

So Anna told her friends about finding the lost coin. Then she said, "I'm going to give a party and you're all invited."

Jesus told a story like this to explain something about heaven. The lost coin is like a person who has done wrong things. But if he is sorry and turns back to God, all the angels in heaven will cheer for joy.

The Son Who Came Home

Jesus was good at telling stories. Once, when he was talking about the importance of forgiving, he told a story about a farmer who had two sons. The sons worked hard every day milking goats, plowing fields, and picking olives. There wasn't much time to enjoy themselves.

One day the youngest son decided that he had had enough. (The Bible doesn't say what his name was, so I shall call him Paul.) He went to his father and said,

"It's time you gave me my share of the farm."

The farmer was to have divided the farm between the two boys when he died. But he agreed to share it right away. When that was done, Paul sold his share, and went off with the money. He was going to travel and have some fun! His brother, who was more responsible, stayed behind to look after the farm.

Weeks and months went by. Paul traveled far, and spent all his money having a good time. Strangely enough, when his money ran out, he lost his friends too.

Now, about that time, there was a terrible drought in the country where he was living. It hadn't rained for years, so nothing would grow and there was hardly any food. For the first time in his life, Paul was poor and hungry. Things got so bad, he had to get a job looking after pigs. The pigs had more to eat than he did!

Paul thought of home, and felt ashamed of himself. He had been very selfish to leave his father and brother.

"My father's servants are better off than I am," he told the pigs.

"I'll go home and tell my father how sorry I am. Perhaps he'll give me some work."

So he set off for the farm. He walked for days and nights, and was still a distance from home, when his father came running towards him. He had spotted Paul up on the hill, and had rushed to meet him. He held his son close to him. Paul was so thin, it was like hugging a bag of bones!

"I'm sorry," said Paul. "I'm not fit to be your son."

His father wouldn't hear another word. Instead he shouted to one of the servants,

"Bring my best coat, a new pair of sandals, and my gold ring."

Then he arranged a big party to celebrate Paul's homecoming. There was music and dancing, and delicious roast meat on the table. Only one person was missing, Paul's older brother. He was still working in the wheat field.

Soon he heard the sound of music and laughter coming from the house, and came to see what was going on. When one of the servants told him that Paul had come home and his father was celebrating, the eldest son was hopping mad. He even refused to go into the house.

"Please come and join us," begged his father.

But his son was in no mood for a party.

"I've worked like a slave on this farm," he shouted. "You've never given *me* a party. Oh no! But when my useless brother comes home, having wasted all his money, you kill the best calf to celebrate!"

You could understand his anger. But his father, who was a loving and forgiving man, saw things differently.

"Everything I have will be yours," he said gently. "You are with me all the time. But Paul was lost, and now he's found. It was as if he had died, and has come back to life. Now, that *is* something worth celebrating."

Jesus and the Children

The disciples were arguing. They believed that soon, Jesus would be crowned king in Jerusalem. But there was something else. Jesus had often spoken about a heavenly kingdom, and some of the disciples were wondering if they would have first place in it. After all, they were his special friends.

They had been strolling by the lake shore, and were still quarreling when they came to Peter's house, in Capernaum. Jesus had walked on ahead, so he didn't know what all the fuss was about. When they came into the house Jesus asked them,

"Why were you arguing?"

The disciples looked a bit embarrassed, and didn't want to tell him. Then one of them got up enough courage to ask,

"Who is the greatest in the kingdom of heaven?"

Jesus had an idea it might be something like that!

"Well," he said, "If you want to be great in my kingdom, you must learn to help others, and put yourselves last."

That made them think. They would have to change their ideas and be less self-important. Just then, a small child ran into the room. Jesus smiled and scooped her up in his arms.

"Let me tell you," he said, "unless you can be like little children, you'll never enter the kingdom of heaven. And anyone who welcomes a child like this, is really welcoming me, and my Father who sent me."

It was a lesson Jesus had to repeat a few days later. He had been busy teaching in the town. It was late afternoon, and Jesus was sitting in the shade of an olive tree. A group of children were playing nearby, having a noisy game of marbles.

The disciples thought the children would disturb Jesus, and wished they would go and play somewhere else! Then one little boy came chasing after his marble. It rolled right up to Jesus. Then all the children came running, and clustered round his feet.

Well, that did it! The disciples got very cross, and tried to send the children away.

But Jesus put out his arms, and said,

"Don't stop them! Let the children come to me. Remember, the kingdom of God belongs to them."

And he blessed each one, before they went off to play.